COTTAGES
CABINS
&
CHALETS

Cottages
CABINS
&
CHALETS

AN OWNER'S GUIDE

FOR GUESTS OF

....

Doubleday Canada Limited / Russet Books

Canadian Cataloguing in Publication Data
Chabanais, Paula
            Cottages, cabins and chalets: an owner's guide for guests
ISBN 0-385-25618-3
1. Vacation homes. I. Coulter, Laurie, 1951-
II. Maher, Peter, 1941-   . III. Title.
HD7289.2C43 1996   643'.2   C96-930575-3

Cover and text design by Peter Maher
Copy editing by Beverley Endersby
Printed and bound in Canada

Packaged by
Russet Books
Division of Paula Chabanais & Associates Limited
17 Russett Avenue
Toronto, Ontario
M6H 3M4

Published in Canada by
Doubleday Canada Limited
105 Bond Street
Toronto, Ontario
M5B 1Y3

Note: The first-aid prevention and treatment information contained in this book is not intended to be substituted for consultation with your physician. All matters pertaining to your health should be directed to a health care professional.

Acknowledgements
The authors would like to thank the many friends and colleagues who gave their encouragement and support, in particular Toronto physician and cottage owner Jean Marmoreo; wildlife biologist Jim Broadfoot; entomologist Paul D. Bell; and long-time cottagers Doug Cruthers, Charis Wahl, David Hamilton, Barbara Boyden, and Jon McKee.

If you have any suggestions for additions to future editions, please contact Russet Books at the above address.

Contents

Sidebars in
light green are
for the owner.

**Sidebars in
dark green are
for guests.**

❏ Boxes are for
the owner to
check off.

Welcome to Our Place

Location: ....

....

....

....

....

Mailing address: ....

....

....

....

History of Our Place

_____

_____

_____

_____

_____

_____

_____

_____

_____

_____

_____

_____

_____

_____

_____

Map to Property

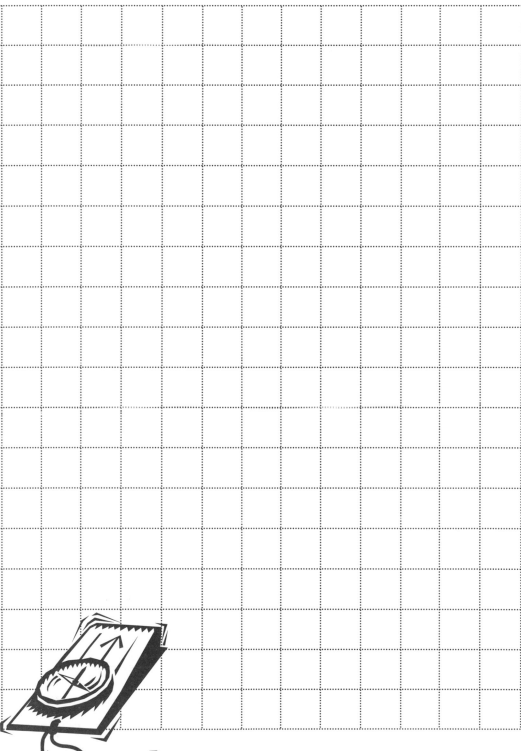

Copy pages 11 and 12 for your guests.

Written Directions

....

....

....

....

....

....

....

....

....

....

....

....

....

Cottage phone number: ....

Map of Property

Indicate property lines, boundary markers, buildings, parking area, closest neighbors.

Phone Numbers

Emergency phone numbers

Ambulance: ....

Hospital: ....

Fire department: ....

Police: ....

Our home phone numbers: ....

....

Our work phone numbers: ....

....

In an emergency, when unable to contact us, please call:

....

Insurance company and cottage or chalet policy number:

....

....

Local phone numbers

Neighbors: ....

....

....

Dentist: ....

Doctor: ....

Drugstore: ....

Electrician: ....

Garage/tow truck: ....

Local lake patrol: ....

Marina: ....

Plumber: ....

Propane supplier: ....

Septic- or holding-tank pumper: ....

Veterinarian: ....

Video store: ....

Other handy numbers: ....

....

....

....

....

....

....

Fire Plan

In the space below, describe what action your guests or tenants should take in case of a fire inside the cottage and ask them to be sure to read your instructions. Plan a way out of every room — the exit may be blocked by flames or smoke — and write down where the outside tap, pails, hoses, and ladders are located. It's also a good idea to include the names and addresses of the nearest neighbors with telephones. If their cottages aren't visible from yours, be sure to include instructions on how to get to them.

....

....

....

....

....

....

....

....

....

....

....

....

....

....

....

....

....

....

....

....

....

....

Fire extinguishers

Extinguishers should be inspected regularly. Read your operator's manual for inspection and servicing information.

Using the wrong type of extinguisher for the fire you are fighting may make the fire worse. For example, using a Class "A" extinguisher or water on a grease or electrical fire is extremely dangerous. Check off the types of extinguishers supplied in the cottage, indicate where they are kept, and encourage your guests or family members to read the directions on the extinguishers.

❏ **Class "A" extinguisher**

Used to fight small fires involving paper, wood, rubbish, curtains, and upholstery.
Location:

....

❏ **Class "B" extinguisher**

Used to fight small fires involving gasoline, fuel oil, cooking oils, paints, solvents, and flammable gases.
Location:

....

❏ **Class "C" extinguisher**

Used to fight small fires involving Class "A" or "B" materials and live electrical power (overheated wiring, stoves, motors, fuse boxes).
Location:

....

❏ **Class "ABC" multipurpose extinguisher**

Used to fight all of the types of fires noted above.
Location:

....

Warning signs of a chimney fire
- sucking sounds
- a loud roar
- a shaking stove pipe

What to do if the chimney catches fire
- Evacuate the building.
- Designate someone to call the fire department.
- Empty an ABC-rated multipurpose extinguisher into the fireplace or woodstove. The chemical travels up the chimney and often extinguishes the flame.
- Watch for sparks or signs of fire on the roof or nearby. Wet the roof and surrounding area with a hose or buckets of water.

Opening-Up Checklist for Guests

The best way to prepare these instructions is to write down each step you take to open up the cottage as you actually complete it. That way you won't miss a step that seems obvious to you but may not be to a guest or tenant.

Opening-Up in the Spring

A spring list is included for those times when it is necessary to ask someone else to take on this chore.

....

....

....

....

....

....

....

....

....

....

....

....

....

....

....

Where We Keep This and That

Write down where everything is on this page and use the numbers to locate items on plan on next two pages.

1 Batteries

....

2 Blankets and pillows (extra)

....

3 Candles

....

4 Equipment manuals

....

5 Fire extinguishers

....

6 First-aid kit

....

7 Flashlight

....

8 Fuses

....

9 Keys

....

10 Lightbulbs

....

11 Matches

....

12 Tool kit, axes, etc.

....

Ground Floor

Second Floor

Guest Checklist

What we'd like you to do and not to do.

Local Etiquette

What our
neighbors
would like you
to do and not
to do.

....

....

....

....

....

....

....

....

....

....

....

....

....

....

....

....

Turning on the Lights

❑ Electrical system

Type of service and restrictions:

....

....

....

....

Replacing a blown fuse:
Turn off the main switch. Turn the blown fuse counter-clockwise to remove. Be sure that the new fuse is the same amperage as the old one. The most common cause of blown fuses is too many appliances operating on the same circuit.

Restoring power to a tripped circuit:
Unplug or switch off extra appliances. Reset circuit breaker to "on."

Fuse box is located:

....

....

What we do when the power goes out:

....

....

....

....

....

❏ Oil lamps

Extra kerosene or lamp oil is kept:

....

If the lamp needs to be filled, it is best to fill it outside. Remove the chimney and fill the fuel reservoir with kerosene or lamp oil. Do not use any other fuel.

To light, turn the wick adjuster until the wick is raised enough for a match to light it. After lighting the wick, quickly place the chimney back on and turn down the wick until the flame stops smoking. To extinguish the flame, cup your hand around the top of the chimney and blow into it.

Keep oil lamps away from high heat and sparks from a wood-burning fire. Put them where they are least likely to be knocked over, and warn children not to touch the chimney, which can become very hot.

Special instructions:

....

....

....

....

....

....

....

....

❏ **Solar system**

A system that makes electricity from sunlight is called a "photovoltaic" (PV) system. How much power the system produces depends upon the number of solar panels and the type and number of batteries.

How to operate our system:

....

....

....

....

....

....

....

....

....

....

....

....

....

Keeping Warm

❑ Fireplace

Tests have shown that a conventional fireplace can actually draw heated air out of the building while it produces only a small amount of heat for the room in which it is located. A firescreen prevents as much as 30% of this heat from entering the room. Be sure to position the screen slightly away from the opening of the fireplace to allow heated air to flow freely over the top of the screen. Although fireplaces are inefficient, most people would agree that they are magical to watch on a chilly evening.

❑ Wood stove

Wood stoves are much more efficient than open fireplaces. Their metal bodies are excellent heat conductors. Be sure to keep the fire small until the stove heats up to prevent the metal from cracking.

Location of wood-stove manual:

....

❑ Fireplace insert

These units operate more like a wood stove than a fireplace. Always burn small, brisk fires in them. The firebox can become very hot.

Wood supply

Our seasoned wood is kept:

....

....

Kindling can be found:

....

....

How to start a wood fire

- Open the fireplace damper or the wood stove's door. The air in the chimney should be flowing upwards. If you feel a cold draft coming down, place a ball of crumpled newspaper up through the damper and light it. In a stove, place the newspaper ball as high up in the stove toward the chimney as you can. The heat from the lit newspaper should warm the chimney and reverse the flow of air.

- Place 3 or 4 sheets of newspaper, which have been balled up fairly tightly, in the firebox or fireplace. Place small pieces of finely split, dry kindling (approximately 10 to 15 pieces) over the paper. Lay the kindling in a crisscross pattern so that there is plenty of air between the pieces. Wood that is stacked too tightly will not burn properly.

- Add 1 or 2 layers of well-spaced, small pieces of wood on top of the kindling and light the paper.

- If you are using a stove, keep the air control fully open at first. The door on some stoves also needs to be left ajar for the first few moments until the chimney is warmed and is producing a strong draft. Don't adjust the air control until you've established a good bed of charcoal.

- If the wood refuses to light and sizzles, it is not properly seasoned. Up to 50% of the weight of a green log is water.

- Keep a "flame" on your fire. A smoldering fire produces pollutants and creosote (tar) in the chimney.

- Add more wood before the fire gets too low.

Cedar, pine, and other softwoods make good kindling.

Special firing instructions for our fireplace or wood stove:

....

....

....

....

....

....

....

....

....

....

....

....

....

....

Safety tips

- Never use gasoline or other flammable liquids to start or restart a fire; the flammable vapors can explode.

- Do not use coal or charcoal in a fireplace or wood stove unless the unit is designed to handle the excess heat and smoke which burning these materials produces.

- Never burn trash or the colored comic sections from newspapers. The colored inks may contain lead, which you don't want to inhale.

- Avoid "roaring" fires. They can start chimney fires in soot and creosote deposits in the flue.

- Always use a firescreen.

- Keep combustible materials — rugs, paper, logs, and kindling — at least 3 feet (1 m) away from the fireplace or stove.

- Wood stoves can become very hot. To reduce the risk of falling against one, be sure no potential tripping hazards are left near it. Don't lean wood against the stove, even to dry it out.

- Be sure the fire is out before retiring for the evening. If the fireplace has glass doors, close them.

- Always shovel ashes into a metal container. Leave the container for a day on a fireproof spot, or douse with water before disposing of the contents.

❏ Wood stove with catalytic combustor

These wood stoves should be operated according to the instructions provided in the owner's manual. Never burn plastic, foil paper, or glossy magazine paper in these appliances. Only unpainted wood and uncolored newspaper should be burned.

The owner's manual for our stove is located

....

or see our directions below:

....

....

....

....

....

....

....

....

....

....

....

❏ High-thermal-mass masonry heater

Although a high-mass heater may look like a conventional fireplace, it operates on a different principle. These heaters store heat in their bricks or stone, which is then radiated to the room. Because they are built differently from a regular masonry fireplace, they have special operating instructions.

Instructions for using our masonry heater:

❑ **Pellet stove**

These stoves burn pellet fuels made from wood or other biomass wastes, such as grain corn.

Special instructions:

....

....

....

....

....

....

....

....

....

....

....

....

....

❏ Kerosene heaters

Portable unvented kerosene heaters can be a potential fire hazard, and the pollutants they produce, particularly carbon monoxide, can represent a significant health hazard. Never place the heater close to paper, curtains, and other readily flammable household materials, and always keep a window open at least an inch (2.5 cm) to provide adequate ventilation in the room where the heater is being used. Turn on only during waking hours, and never leave the heater untended. Add the kerosene to the heater outside, and refuel after the device has cooled. It is dangerous to substitute other fuels for kerosene in these heaters.

The owner's manual for our heater is located

....

or see our directions below:

....

....

....

....

....

....

....

....

Kerosene should be stored in a metal fuel container marked "Kerosene" and painted green, or some color other than red, so that your guests won't accidentally confuse it with a container of gasoline. It should not be stored inside the cottage.

❏ Propane space heaters

Propane needs air to burn. Always open a window when using a space heater. Before lighting it, sniff all around the area, particularly at floor level. If you smell boiled cabbage or rotten eggs, the propane tank may be leaking. These odors are added to the fuel to warn you about leaks. If you smell gas, don't light the appliance.

The owner's manual for our heater is located

....

 or see our directions below:

....

....

....

....

....

....

....

Warning signs of carbon-monoxide poisoning

Carbon monoxide is an invisible, colorless, odorless gas created when fossil fuels burn incompletely. It replaces oxygen in the bloodstream, eventually causing suffocation. Early carbon-monoxide poisoning symptoms include dizziness, weakness, headache, drowsiness, and/or nausea. More serious poisoning leads to difficulty breathing, and even death.

❏ Electric heaters

Portable electric heaters can be fire hazards. Keep them 3 feet (1 m) away from combustible materials, and never leave them on when you leave the house or go to bed.

Special instructions:

....

....

....

....

....

....

....

....

❏ Electric blankets

Although these blankets are wonderfully toasty on cold nights, they are electrical appliances and come with the requisite do's and don'ts. Don't tuck in or fold over the wired area of the blanket. To prevent damage to the wiring, don't lie on top of the blanket or put anything heavy on it. Do turn it off when the blanket is not in use. And do pull out the plug during an electrical storm. One cottager received the shock of his life when lightning struck a tall pine next to his cottage and entered the building's electrical grid. He found himself sandwiched between the wiring in the blanket and the metal bedsprings. Needless to say, it was a tingly experience, one he doesn't want to repeat.

See pages 100 to 102 for first-aid treatment of sunburn, heat exhaustion, and sunstroke.

Keeping Cool

How we keep our cottage cool in hot weather:

....

....

....

....

....

....

....

....

....

....

....

....

....

....

Hot-weather tips

- Drink plenty of water throughout the day.

- Avoid too much sunshine. Sunburn slows the skin's ability to cool itself.

- Wear lightweight, light-colored clothing that reflects heat and sunlight.

- Wear a wide-brimmed hat to protect your face and head.

- Limit your intake of alcoholic beverages. Although beer and alcoholic beverages appear to satisfy thirst, they actually cause further body dehydration on hot days.

- Eat well-balanced, light meals.

Never eat
berries or
mushrooms
unless you are
sure they are
edible.

Cottage Cooking

Where to shop

....

....

....

....

....

....

Where to forage

....

....

....

....

....

....

....

Fishing spots

Local fishing seasons and licenses:

For those of you who have two-burners-and-the-oven-work-but-not-both-at-the-same-time kind of cottage stoves.

❏ **Electric stove**

Special instructions:

....

....

....

❏ **Woodburning cookstove**

Special instructions:

....

....

....

....

....

....

....

....

....

....

....

❏ Naphtha or propane cook stove

Propane and napththa need air to burn. Because they consume oxygen, these appliances should *never* be used in unventilated or enclosed areas.

Special instructions:

....

....

....

❏ Propane refrigerator

Special instructions:

....

....

....

If you smell boiled cabbage or rotten eggs, propane may be leaking from a cylinder. These odors are added to the fuel to warn you about leaks. If you smell one of these odors, turn off the cylinder valve and leave the immediate area. Let the area ventilate before re-entering.

❏ Electric refrigerator

Special instructions:

....

....

....

Your propane fridge's burner and flue may become blocked if the refrigerator has been turned off or moved, or after one year of use. This may result in carbon monoxide being produced. A trained technician should inspect and clean your fridge once a year to make sure this doesn't happen.

Always place
the barbecue
in an open,
well-ventilated
space away
from trees,
brush, etc.
Keep a fire
extinguisher
handy at all
times.

Barbecues

There are two main points to remember when barbecuing: The food must be cooked over a bed of hot coals with no flame. And foods must not be allowed to dry out. Meat and fish need marinating and/or basting.

Barbecue equipment

- table or flat surface
- skewers
- wire brush
- carryall for spices
- metal lifter
- basting brush
- gloves
- tongs
- spray bottle for water

❏ Traditional barbecue

Here are two ways to light a traditional barbecue:

- Pierce a large can with holes and fill with briquettes.

- Place the can in the barbecue and soak the briquettes with barbecue starter. Leave for ten minutes or so and then light with a match or taper. When they are glowing, empty briquettes into the barbecue, using a glove, and cover with more briquettes.

- Or insert an electric starter beneath the briquettes and then plug in. When briquettes are glowing, remove starter. Do not use liquid barbecue starter with this method.

❏ Gas barbecue

Location of gas barbecue manual:

....

How to light our barbecue:

....

....

....

....

....

....

....

....

....

....

....

Cheap leather or canvas work gloves last longer than designer oven gloves for barbecuing.

Marinades

Meat and fish should be left in a marinade made without oil for 4 to 8 hours. Baste meat or fish with a mixture of the marinade and oil (1 part oil to 2 parts marinade), using a wide brush.

Recipes

Burger ideas

Additions to hamburger patties:
- minced onion
- minced green pepper
- dry mustard

- tomato sauce
- ground cumin
- Tabasco sauce

- jerk seasoning
- ketchup

Toppings:
- cheese slices
- pickles
- veggies (lettuce, tomato, onion)
- pineapple
- relish, ketchup, mustard
- hot peppers

Vegetables in foil pouches

Vegetables can be cooked on a barbecue in a foil pouch.
- Prepare foil pouch by doubling up two sheets of aluminum foil. Insert vegetables, sprinkle with water, and seal with a triple fold. It is important to make the pouch as airtight as possible.
- Carrots and squash are particularly tasty cooked this way.

Jim McConnell's barbecued lamb

Serves 4

1	garlic clove	1
1	2-lb (1-kg) deboned leg of lamb	1
1 cup	fresh mint	250 mL

- Cut garlic into slivers and insert into slits made in outside of lamb.
- Coarsely chop mint and sprinkle over meat.
- Carefully wrap lamb in foil and seal.
- Cook on barbecue for 1-1/4 hours. Turn every 15 minutes. For the last 15 minutes, open pouch.

Note: This recipe can also be used when cooking over an open fire, using a rack. Remember that the fire should be mainly embers with little or no flame.

Barbecued chicken on a spit

Serves 4

1	chicken
1 bunch	sweet herbs: tarragon, celery, green onions
	Barbecue Sauce (see page 50)

- Tie bunch of sweet herbs together and insert into chicken cavity.
- Skewer or tie wings and legs close to body.
- Put chicken on spit and baste frequently with Barbecue Sauce. Chicken is done when leg feels loose when wiggled, roughly 20 minutes per pound or 40 minutes per kilogram at 350° F (180° C).

Frozen shrimps sprinkled with a little lemon juice and cooked in foil for about 10 minutes make a delicious appetizer.

Barbecue sauce

1/2 cup	ketchup	125 mL
1/2 cup	water	125 mL
1/4 cup	white vinegar	60 mL
1/8–1/2 cup	vegetable oil	25–125 mL
1/4 cup	chopped onion	60 mL
1/4 cup	chopped green pepper	60 mL
1	clove garlic, minced	1
1/2 tsp	brown sugar	2 mL
1/2 tsp	salt	2 mL
1/2 tsp	celery seed	2 mL
2 tsp	paprika	10 mL
1 tbsp	Worcestershire sauce	15 mL
A few drops	Tabasco sauce	A few drops

- Combine ingredients in a saucepan, bring to a boil and simmer for 15 minutes. Use more oil for basting chicken than for basting pork or beef.

Our Favorite Recipes

Our Favorite Recipes

Our Favorite Recipes

Our Favorite Recipes

Our Favorite Recipes

Campfires for Roasting Marshmallows and Other Good Things

Preparing the site

Select a site within easy access to water, on bedrock or sand, and sheltered from the prevailing wind. It should be at least 10 feet (3 m) from any wood, tree roots, overhanging branches, or bushes, and 50 feet (15 m) from any building. Clear pine needles, grass, twigs, and leaves in an 8-foot (2-m) circle around your campfire site. Scrape away any soil to rock or sand, and build the campfire following the diagram below.

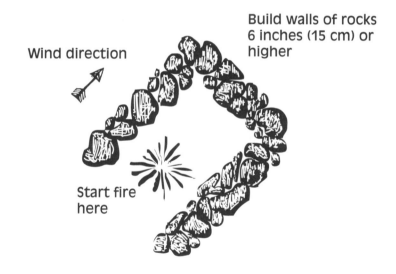

Wind direction

Build walls of rocks
6 inches (15 cm) or
higher

Start fire
here

Basic safety rules

- Keep your fire small.

- Never leave your fire unattended.

- Drown the fire thoroughly before leaving the site.

- Stir the ashes to uncover any hot coals.

- Drown the fire again.

Where we have campfires:

....

....

....

....

....

Open-fire regulations in our area:

....

....

....

....

....

....

Garbage Disposal

❏ Garbage pickup

Day of week: ....

Special instructions:

....

....

....

....

❏ Local dump

Location of dump:

....

....

....

Open (days and times):

....

County or municipal dump card is located:

....

....

....

If you are leaving for home before the dump opens, please don't leave garbage at the dump gates. Take it with you.

❏ **Bins for recyclables at local dump**

Special instructions:

....

....

....

❏ **Cottage compost bin**

Location of kitchen compost container:

....

....

Location of compost bin:

....

- What can go in the composter: vegetables, fruit
  (chop up large pieces), coffee grounds, tea leaves,
  egg shells.
- What can't go in the composter: meat, bones, fish
  scraps, fat, oil, milk products, pet droppings.

Special instructions:

....

....

....

....

Check box if
animal or
insect is
present in your
area.

Pesky Pests

Mammals

❏ **Bats**

Bats are not rodents, are not blind, and won't get tangled in your hair. They eat thousands of insects. That said, it is a little disconcerting having one flapping around in a room.

The primary goal of a bat that has strayed inside is to escape. It will often leave on its own if a door or window is left open. If it doesn't, a bat can be caught in flight with a net; or, when it lands, cover it with a large can, slip a piece of cardboard underneath, and then release it outside. Bats are gentle animals, even when chased; however, they can carry rabies and should not be handled with bare hands.

❏ **Bears**

Phone number of government or private animal-removal service:

....

Bears that want to eat humans are very rare. Bears that want to eat our food are another matter, particularly when berry crops are poor. In bear country, it's a good idea to keep food and garbage inside. Barbecue grills should be washed after every use and, if a fish has been cleaned outside, be sure to dispose of the evidence promptly.

Close encounters of the bear kind: At your cabin, scare a bear away by banging pot lids together from a safe place. If you surprise a bear in the woods, it will likely try to get away from you as quickly as it can. If it does approach or stand on its hind legs to get a better look at you, it may be curious, not aggressive. Your reaction should be to act like a human animal rather than one of its prey animals. Running may trigger an instinctive reaction to chase you, and since a bear can outrun an Olympic sprinter, it won't be much of a contest. Stand tall, speak in a loud low voice,

back away slowly and diagonally, and avoid direct eye contact with the animal.

A bear that is protecting a food source or its young may warn you to leave the area by flattening its ears, snorting, and making a short charge at you. If this happens, follow the above instructions, but act aggressively by standing your ground, shouting, and waving your arms. Almost all charges are bluff charges.

❏ Porcupines

It's a myth that a porcupine can throw any of its 30,000 barbed quills at you. These slow-moving, usually nocturnal animals are only a nuisance when they begin gnawing on the floor joists of buildings or the outhouse toilet seat.

If your dog has an altercation with a porcupine, the quills can be pulled out with pliers. Cut the ends off first to release the vacuum. However, if there are quills inside your pet's mouth, there are a great many of them on its head or body, or a quill breaks off when you try to extract it, a visit to the local vet is in order.

❏ Raccoons

Raccoons have been known to open screen doors and wander into vacation homes looking for food. Their almost handlike front paws can also open garbage cans and latches. Avoid leaving full garbage bags outside, keep garbage can lids firmly shut, and lock boxes and outbuildings where trash is kept.

If you're tempted to feed these cute-looking animals by hand, please don't. They can be carriers of rabies. In addition, once they associate the cottage with a ready food supply, they will return time and time again.

❏ Skunks

Skunks use their spray for defending themselves, not for attacking. The spray can reach a perceived enemy standing 10 to 15 feet (3 to 5 m) away, so it's best to give these small animals a wide berth.

If your pet is sprayed by a skunk, bathe it in tomato juice or in equal parts vinegar and water. Rub into fur, let stand, then wash with soap and water. The odor won't completely disappear but will be more tolerable. If you think the spray has gotten into your pet's eyes, flush several times with water and take your animal to the local vet.

Rodents

❏ Mice

Mice can survive almost anywhere — they've been found nibbling the supplies used on polar expeditions — and it's a rare cottage or cabin that hasn't been paid a visit. If you hear the sound of scurrying feet in the night or find mouse droppings in the morning, be sure to put food away in gnaw-proof containers, clean and disinfect counters, sweep or vacuum floors often, and wash the dishes.

If you open up a cottage and find large numbers of droppings, be careful cleaning up. Some rodents are carriers of hantavirus, which in humans may cause flu-like illness progressing to acute respiratory distress. People can be exposed to this virus by inhalation of contaminated dust, contact between broken skin and material contaminated by rodent excreta, or possibly ingestion of contaminated food or water. To clean up, wear latex or rubber gloves and a dust mask, and clean affected areas with general household disinfectant solutions or bleach and water. Chances of getting Hantavirus Pulmonary Syndrome are very low, but it's wise to take precautions.

Here are a few tips for mouse-catchers. Crunchy peanut butter, chocolate, cheese, raisins, and cotton for nesting material work well as bait. Place traps near walls or in corners. Wear gloves or use tongs when disposing of a spring-loaded trap and caught mouse.

Our mouse-catching method:

....

....

....

....

Reptiles, amphibians, and invertebrates

❏ **Venomous snakes**
Nearest medical center with anti-venom serum:

....

Northern North America's venomous snakes — the rattlesnake, cottonmouth, and copperhead — are all pit vipers. These snakes have triangle-shaped heads with a pit on each side between the eye and nostril. They are not aggressive animals, although they will defend themselves if threatened or injured. Nor are they particularly numerous, so there is little chance of seeing one, let alone of being bitten.

❏ **Rattlesnakes**
All rattlesnakes have a rattle at the end of their tails, but because the various species are different sizes, the sound the rattle makes varies. It has been likened to a buzzing noise or the sound made by cicadas or escaping steam.

A few precautions: Look before you stick your hands under a log or into a hole where a snake may be hidden. When out walking, look down frequently at your path to avoid stepping on a rattler. If you think you hear one, don't move until you determine where the sound is coming from. You don't want to step on the rattlesnake or move into its range. Never handle a freshly killed snake; even decapitated heads have been known to bite!

In snake country, the first rule is to learn to distinguish those snakes that are poisonous from those that aren't. Every year harmless snakes swish their tails on some dry leaves and are killed because they are mistaken for rattlers. For your guests' peace of mind and to protect your area's snakes, it's a good idea to have a snake identification guide in the bookcase, with the local snakes checked off.

See page 96 for advice on snake bites and page 98 for jellyfish stings.

❑ Copperheads
❑ Cottonmouths
When alarmed, these snakes may also vibrate their tails. Bites usually occur when hikers unknowingly step on or touch unseen copperheads or cottonmouths. For this reason, the same precautions you would take in rattlesnake country should be taken in areas where these snakes live.

❑ Snapping turtles
These freshwater turtles, which weigh 10 to 35 pounds (5 to 16 kg) on average, have big heads; small lower shells; and long, saw-toothed tails. Children should be told to keep away from snapping turtles; as their name suggests, their jaws are very powerful.

❑ Jellyfish
Various species of these gelatinous, umbrella-shaped animals — one is aptly called the moon jelly — are found offshore along the coasts of North America. Onshore winds will sometimes blow them ashore. Their stinging tentacles should be avoided.

❑ Leeches
Leeches are ugly but harmless little creatures. In North America, only one allergic reaction to a bite has ever been recorded. If you have trouble flicking a leech off your skin or a squeamish child's, try sprinkling it with salt or vinegar. An ice cube can also be effective.

Insects and ticks

❏ Ants

If ants are discovered indoors, they have come looking for food and found it. If none is available, they'll simply leave again. Put away all food after use and thoroughly clean all areas where ants are congregating with a solution of equal parts vinegar and water. If you can see where they're entering the cottage, sprinkling red chili pepper or paprika across their line of entry is said to be a good temporary solution. Squeezing lemon juice in the hole and putting lemon peel across the entrance is also said to work. And there are always ant traps, which can be bought at grocery and hardware stores.

❏ Black flies

Time of year in our area:

....

These tiny insects have a stout, hump-backed appearance. The bad news is that they like sunny, hot days just as much as we do. The good news is that they don't bite at night outdoors and seldom at any time indoors. They are most active early in the morning and late in the afternoon.

Black flies aren't fussy about which part of your body they attack, although they seem to favor the head, just under the rim of your hat. Dark colors attract them, so wear light-colored clothing with tight-fitting cuffs during black-fly season.

❏ Deer and horse flies

Time of year in our area:

....

Unlike mosquitoes and black flies, these large (1/4- to 1-inch/0.5- to 2.5-cm-long), big-headed flies have good eyesight and are attracted by movement. Sweat also attracts them. They tend to be most bothersome on hot, dry days.

One of the best ways to control insects is to retain the natural environment around your cottage. A lot with a lawn and most of the natural land and water vegetation removed is not suitable habitat for dragonflies, birds, and other natural predators of biting insects.

See pages 98
and 99 for
first-aid
treatment of
spider, tick,
and insect
bites.

To be a pest yourself and for some temporary relief from
these insects, walk slowly up to someone in your group,
then duck and run backwards a few steps. Your victim will
inherit your bugs!

❑ **Deer ticks**
Any season of the year except during periods of subfreez-
ing temperatures.

Has Lyme disease been reported in this area?
Yes ❑   No ❑

Ticks require a blood meal at the larva, nymph, and adult
stages of their life cycle. If a tick's host is infected with the
bacterium that causes Lyme disease, the tick will become
infected as well and pass along the infection to future
hosts. The tick must feed for 10 or more hours before the
disease is transmitted. The nymph, about the size of a
poppy seed, can easily go undetected and is responsible for
most Lyme disease cases in humans. The adult tick is the
size of a sesame seed, oval-shaped and wingless. After feeding, it is the size of a small pea and blue-black in color.

Deer ticks are found in woods and grassy areas where
deer and field mice thrive. It is impossible for ticks to find
their way to you by flying or hopping; you must come in
contact with them by brushing up against low bushes or
tall grass where they wait for animals to pass by. Wear
light-colored, long-sleeved shirts, and pants tucked into
socks when walking in tick-prone areas. Light colors do
not repel ticks but simply allow you to spot them more
easily on your clothing. Always inspect your clothing and
body for ticks when you return to the cottage from a walk
in the woods.

❏ **Mosquitoes**

Time of year in our area:

....

Larger than black flies, mosquitoes are long-legged, fragile-looking insects with a long proboscis, which the females use to extract three times their own weight in blood from their victims. They bite anywhere, anytime, although they seem to be most active at dawn and dusk and on overcast and humid days.

   In mosquito season, wear pastel-colored clothing and resist the urge to bat off the hordes with your hands. Skeeters are attracted to dark colors as well as to high body temperature, perspiration, and carbon dioxide produced by nervous people.

❏ **No-see-ums**

Time of year in our area:

....

These biting midges — also called punkies or sand flies — are less than 1/16 inch (1.5 mm) long. Because they are so tiny, they can easily fly inside through ordinary window screens. They seldom bite on windy days but seem to be particularly active at dusk. Like mosquitoes, they are attracted by high body temperatures, so flailing arms and jumping up and down will do more harm than good. Wear clothes made of tightly woven cloth — they can wriggle through loose weaves. Zippers are better than buttons, and tight cuffs better than loose ones.

❏ **Stable flies**

Time of year in our area:

....

Stable flies are a bit smaller than a standard house fly. They are often found around beaches, where the larvae feed on decaying vegetation. The adults have piercing mouthparts which inflict a painful bite, usually on the ankles.

Removing dying vegetation around the cottage will help keep the number of these flies down.

Insect repellents

Most insect repellents that are applied to the skin work for from one to several hours, but because they can be removed by swimming, perspiration, and evaporation, they must be reapplied to maintain effectiveness. The best topical repellents contain N, N-diethyl-m-toluamide, commonly called DEET. DEET repels mosquitoes, black flies, ticks, and no-see-ums. It is less effective against deer and horse flies and is ineffective against bees and wasps.

Repellents containing higher-percentage solutions of DEET are not more repellent. They simply last longer, although studies have suggested that a 30% solution lasts almost as long as a 90% solution. DEET is absorbed through the skin and may cause allergic and toxic reactions, especially when used on the skin repeatedly in high concentrations. It should never be used on children.

Oil of citronella–based repellents provide short-term protection against mosquitoes and black flies, but are probably not effective against ticks. Avon's Skin So Soft, a concentrated bath oil, is sometimes used as a repellent. Like citronella products, it repels bugs for a much shorter period of time than DEET repellents, and the safety of repeated applications is unknown.

Many people put repellent on their clothing rather than on their skin.

"Citrosa" plants have been advertised in Canada and the United States as "guaranteed to repel mosquitoes," but studies have shown that no plant will repel skeeters just sitting in a pot. Vitamin B and garlic remedies have also failed scientific bug-repelling tests.

Our best skeeter-skeedaddler remedies:

....

....

....

....

....

....

....

....

....

....

....

....

....

....

....

What not to
flush down the
toilet or drain:
bleach, chemical
cleansers,
barbecue starter,
drain openers,
kitchen fat and
grease, facial
tissues, tampons,
cigarette butts,
nail-polish
remover; in fact,
anything that
doesn't break
down naturally.

Plumbing Primer

❏ Septic system
❏ Holding tank

Practicing water conservation is an even better idea at the cottage or chalet than it is in town. Too much water isn't healthy for septic systems and rapidly fills holding tanks. Some people follow the old rule, "If it's yellow, let it mellow. If it's brown, flush it down."

Our rules:

....

....

Signs of septic-system failure:
- a smelly black liquid backing up in drains or toilets
- liquid waste seeping to the surface near the septic-system field
- disagreeable odors around the cottage or chalet
- extremely slow flushing of toilet

What to do if the system is not working:

....

....

....

....

....

....

....

....

....

....

....

....

What to do if the holding-tank alarm goes off:
If the holding-tank alarm goes off, there may be a fault in
the alarm system or the tank may need to be pumped out.

....

....

....

....

....

....

....

....

It's a good idea to keep the manual near the toilet. If it has disappeared, be sure to write down operating instructions, what can and cannot go into the toilet, and cleaning methods.

❏ Incinerating, composting, or chemical toilet

Instructions:

....

....

....

....

....

....

....

....

....

....

....

....

....

❑ Outhouse

To control odors, some cottagers use small quantities of a type of lime known as calcium hydroxide, and others use ash from the fireplace or wood stove.

Instructions:

....

....

....

....

....

....

....

....

....

....

....

....

....

....

....

❏ **Water pump**

If turning on the taps produces no water at all, check to see that the pump switch is in the "on" position and that the fuse hasn't blown. If the pump doesn't shut off, be sure that a tap hasn't been left on or that the toilet isn't running.

Our pump's idiosyncrasies:

....

....

....

....

....

....

....

....

....

....

....

....

❏ Drinking-water supply

What we do:

....

....

....

....

....

....

....

....

....

....

....

....

....

....

Water brought from home should be kept in the refrigerator and used within a few days.

75

Washing Clothes

❏ Washing machine

To prevent overloading the septic system, do small loads throughout the week. Phosphate-free detergent should be used.

Special instructions:

....

....

....

....

....

❏ Drier

Special instructions:

....

....

....

....

....

....

....

❑ Line and clothes pins

Location:

....

❑ Laundromat

Directions to the nearest laundromat:

....

....

....

....

....

....

....

....

....

....

Best time to go:

....

....

Washing Bodies

Our hot-water system (how it works and size of tank):

....

....

....

....

....

....

....

❏ Indoor shower

To conserve water, limit shower time and turn off water while soaping up or shampooing. Clean stall with an environmentally friendly cleaner.

....

....

....

....

....

❏ **Outdoor shower**

How ours works:

....

....

....

....

....

....

❏ Bathtub

Baths use more water than showers, so use the shower more frequently than the bath to conserve water. Clean with an environmentally friendly cleaner.

Everyday ablutions

To conserve water, turn off water while shaving and brushing teeth.

Is the tap water safe for brushing teeth?
❏ Yes ❏ No

Bathing in lake or river

The environmentally correct way to bathe in a lake or river is to jump in, jump out, soap up with biodegradable soap, rinse off with a pail of water away from shore, and jump in again.

All-purpose cleaner:
4 tbsp (50 mL) baking soda mixed with 1 quart (1 L) warm water
or
baking soda used on a damp sponge

Boats and Floats

❏ Small boats (17 ft/5 m)

Basic equipment for small boats:

- one PFD or lifejacket per person
- an effective sound signalling device (whistle, horn)
- bailer
- sponge
- spare paddle
- fire extinguisher if boat has inboard motor or fixed fuel tank
- flashlight if not equipped with running lights

Storage directions for small boats and equipment:

....

....

....

....

....

....

....

....

....

....

❏ **Motorboats**

Make of motor: ....

Serial number: ....

Operating directions for our motorboats:

....

....

....

....

Where to buy gas:

....

....

....

Mooring directions:

....

....

....

....

....

....

Safety rules

- Make sure an outboard motor is set in neutral and in the straight-ahead position before starting it.

- Make sure the gas tank isn't empty.

- Do not smoke near gas.

- A motorboat must slow down when passing sail-boats, rowboats, and canoes.

- Keep right (when boats are approaching head on). Give right (when paths will cross, vessel on right has right of way). Big is right (when a freighter or ferry boat cannot maneuver, it has the right of way).

- Red right returning. Keep all red buoys, beacons, and lights on your right when going upstream or going into port.

- Head for shore when a storm threatens.

- Children in boats without adults should stay in sight of the cottage.

- Before you leave the dock, let someone know where you are going and when you plan to return.

- When cruising, keep the boat 100 ft (30 m) offshore to prevent the wake from damaging docks and moored boats and to avoid swimmers.

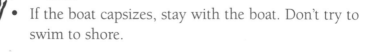

- If the boat capsizes, stay with the boat. Don't try to swim to shore.

Lifejackets and PFDs

Keyhole and vest lifejackets are designed to turn an *unconscious* person in the water from the face-down position to the face-up position. PFDs, on the other hand, are designed to keep a *conscious* person afloat. They will not necessarily turn a person over. When choosing a lifejacket or PFD for yourself or your child, always check the weight range on the inside label.

To test a PFD or lifejacket, put it on, wade into waist-deep water, bend your knees, and float on your back. Make sure that the device keeps your chin above water and that you can breathe easily. Practice swimming on your front and on your back.

If your lifejackets or PFDs do not have a whistle, attach a small plastic one to the zippers.

Knots

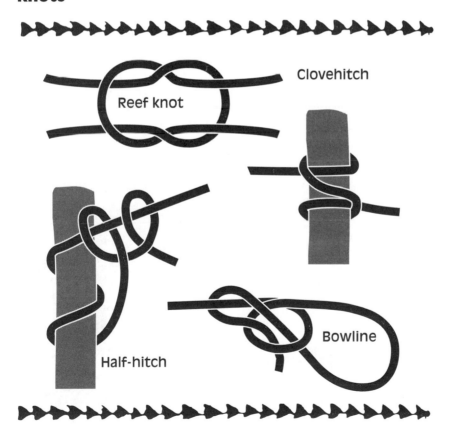

Reef knot

Clovehitch

Half-hitch

Bowline

Map of lake, river, or oceanfront

Indicate hazards, channels, currents, prevailing winds, etc. on this map.

Swimming and water play

Safety rules:
- Only plastic glasses and plates should be used on the dock or beach.
- Check swimming area for underwater hazards.
- Protect your head and spine; don't dive into unfamiliar waters. Feet first first time.
- Always swim with a buddy; never swim alone.
- Children should always be supervised by a responsible adult.
- Don't swim after dark.
- Don't rely on flotation devices such as rafts or air mattresses.
- Alcohol and swimming do not mix.
- If caught in an ocean rip-tide or a river current, swim diagonally until free.
- Never turn your back on the ocean — high waves can appear without warning.

Water and beach fun:
Tag, treasure hunts, and catch can be played in the water. Basketball can be played using a beachball and an old tire or inner tube as the hoop. Toy boats can be made out of pieces of bark and twigs, or milk cartons cut in half. Skipping stones, making sand sculptures, and searching for shells are enjoyable at any age.

Where we keep our water and beach toys:

....

....

....

....

....

Weather Watch

Weather forecasting

Weather systems in North America move from west to east. High, wispy cirrus clouds ("mares' tails") are often the first sign of rain. As the warm, moist air of a warm front moves in, lower altocumulus clouds ("flocks of sheep") are seen. The clouds get thicker until the sky is completely overcast and rain begins. Towering, dense cumulonimbus clouds are a sign of thunderstorms.

The following old-fashioned weather maxims do seem to have some scientific basis:

"A ring around the moon means rain is on the way."

"If there is frost or dew, or morning fog,
No rain this day will you log."

"When wind is in the east,
'Tis good for neither man or beast."

"Red sky at night, sailors delight,
Red sky in the morning, sailors take warning."

Our own weather maxims:

....

....

....

....

....

Storm warnings

What to do before a thunderstorm hits:
Pull small boats well up on shore and tie them up. Put all loose objects on the dock and outside (lawn chairs, lifejackets, paddles, etc.) away.

During a thunderstorm:
Stay indoors. Do not handle any electrical equipment or use the telephone. Avoid bathtubs, water faucets, and sinks because metal pipes can transmit electricity.

Our own instructions regarding boats, etc.:

....

....

....

....

....

....

....

....

....

....

....

Rainy-Day Activities

Cards

Playing cards are kept:

....

"Pig" is a game for from 3 to 13 children and/or adults. A pack of cards is divided up into denominations, 4 cards for each player; for example, 6 players would use 4 aces, 4 kings, 4 queens, 4 jacks, 4 tens, and 4 nines. The dealer deals 4 cards to each player. The object of the game is to be the first to make 4 of a kind and not to be the last to notice when someone else does.

To begin the game, the players look at their hands and then pass 1 card to the player on their left. This continues until a player has 4 cards of the same denomination. He immediately stops passing cards and puts his finger to his nose. The other players also put their fingers to their noses. The last one to do this is the Pig.

Board games

Board games are kept:

....

....

If no board games are to be found, in a pinch you can make a checkerboard (8 squares across and 8 squares down) on a sheet of paper and use 12 dimes and 12 nickels, or cookies of different colors or shapes, for checkers.

Jigsaw puzzles

Puzzles are kept:

....

You can help children make their own jigsaw puzzles by pasting pictures out of magazines onto cardboard squares and cutting them into puzzle pieces.

Pantomime and puppet shows

Charades is a good game for a rainy day. Divide into two teams. Each player on one team is given a subject written on a slip of paper by the opposing team. It could be a movie, TV, or book title. The player then acts out the title, hoping that his or her teammates can guess it before the time is up. Signs can be used; for example, to indicate the number of words in a title, hold up the same number of fingers. A small word can be indicated by placing your thumb and index finger close together. "Rhymes with" is indicated by tugging your ear. The team to guess the most subjects in the least amount of time wins.

Even if you've forgotten to bring puppets, your children can put on a puppet show using figures cut out of paper and attached with tape to sticks. A table can be made into a stage, props can be made out of cardboard or play dough, and flashlights used for lights. No script is necessary. Just make it up as you go along. The kids in one family hold a puppet show based on their favorite movie each summer.

Kitchen fun

Making monster cookies, mini pizzas with lots of different toppings to choose from, Dagwood sandwiches, or imaginative drinks can make the time pass quickly on a dreary day. Face sandwiches are always a hit with younger kids. Spread a slice of bread with margarine, butter, cream cheese, or peanut butter for skin. Add grated carrots or shredded cheese for hair; round pickles, banana rings, or olives for eyes; a banana slice, pickle, or green pepper for a nose; raisins or red pepper for a mouth.

Crafts

Nature art:
Before it really starts to pour, collect burrs, thistles, pine cones, bark, seeds, sticks, dried grass, and shells. You can make animals or imaginary creatures from the burrs, thistles, and pine cones, and a collage with the other objects. Or collect rocks and paint them. Or make sand paintings using sand tinted with food coloring and sprinkled on cardboard painted with white glue.

Papier-mâché head:
You will need a balloon, lots of newspaper torn into strips, a large dish, 1-3/4 cups (400 mL) white flour, 2-1/2 cups (600 mL) warm water, waxed paper, paints, brushes, and glue. Put the flour in the dish and add the warm water. Mix into a smooth paste. Blow up the balloon and tie off the end. Paste the strips of newspaper onto the balloon until it is completely covered. Put about 10 more layers of newspaper onto the first layer. Use more paper and paste to make the nose, ears, and mouth of a person, monster, or animal. Let dry for two days, and then paint the head and decorate with whatever you can find — string, colored paper, etc.

Singsongs

For instruments, you can use spoons, pots and pans, sticks, rattles, and glasses. Here are the lyrics for some rounds, in case you've forgotten the words:

Canoe Song

My paddle's keen and bright, Flashing with silver
Follow the wild goose flight, Dip, dip and swing.

Dip, dip and swing her back, Flashing with silver
Swift as the wild goose flies, Dip, dip and swing.

Fire's Burning

Fire's burning, Fire's burning. Draw nearer, Draw nearer.
In the gloaming, In the gloaming, Come sing and be merry.

Frère Jacques

Frère Jacques, Frère Jacques
Dormez-vous? Dormez-vous?
Sonnez les matines! Sonnez les matines!
Din, din, don. Din, din, don.

Are you sleeping? Are you sleeping?
Brother John, Brother John?
Morning bells are ringing. Morning bells are ringing.
Ding, ding, dong. Ding, ding, dong.

Singing glasses:

Use 5 tall glasses. Leave one empty, fill the second 1/4 full
of water, the third 1/2 full, the fourth 3/4 full, and the fifth
to the top of the glass. Lightly tap the rims with a teaspoon
to play a tune.

Books and magazines

Location of local library:

....

Location of local bookstore:

....

Location of store with best magazine rack:

....

Rattles: Fill empty juice cans with pebbles or dried beans and tape the ends shut.

Videos

Location of local video store:

....

....

....

Radio and TV stations

Call numbers for favorite stations:

....

....

....

....

Movies

Location of local cinema:

....

....

Bowling alley

Location of local bowling alley:

....

....

Other places to visit on a rainy day

....

....

....

....

....

....

....

What we like to do on rainy days

....

....

....

....

....

....

First Aid and Prevention

General first aid

A word about shock

Shock can occur, to some degree, after any injury, so it's good to know what to look for and what not to do; for example, never give a person in severe shock anything to eat or drink. If the victim has lost consciousness, seek medical help immediately.

Look for these symptoms of shock:

- Victim may look dazed and confused.

- Victim may be either pale or flushed, depending on the type of injury.

- Victim's breathing may be irregular and/or weak.

- Victim may be vomiting.

Until medical help arrives, do the following:

- Have the victim lie down on his or her back; keep the head level with the body or slightly elevated.

- Do not let the head go lower than the body.

- Loosen tight clothing at the chest and neck.

- If the skin is pale and cool, provide warmth, but be careful not to overheat.

- If the skin is hot and red, apply bath towels soaked in cool water until the skin returns to normal temperature, and then provide warmth.

Sprains and breaks

- Use ice compress, if available, for 20 minutes to control swelling. Elevate sprained limb.

- Repeat, using ice water or cold compresses, every 4 hours until the swelling has stopped.

Fractures

These must always receive immediate medical attention.

- If you even suspect injury to the neck or spine, *do not* move the person at all — get medical help.

- To avoid further injury: immobilize limb with split or sling.

- If the fracture is compound (the bone is sticking out of the skin), take measures to stop bleeding while you get medical help.

Burns

Dry burns and scalds are the most common type of burns. If you are in any doubt about the severity of a burn, or the victim is an infant or a sick or elderly person, immediately seek professional attention.

Tiny burns or scalds can usually be treated on site by:

- cooling the burned area, usually by gently flooding with cold water;
- preventing infection;
- relieving pain.

Never put anyone at risk or delay getting medical attention by trying to capture or kill the animal.

Animal bites

- Control bleeding with tourniquet, if necessary.

- Flush the wound immediately to remove saliva, and cleanse thoroughly with mild soap and cool water for 5 minutes.

- Flush with cool, running water.

- Cover with a sterile pad or clean cloth, and seek medical attention.

- Instruct the victim not to move the affected area until a doctor has been consulted.

Snake bites

Poisonous or nonpoisonous snake bites should have medical attention *immediately*. The victim should be taken to a hospital as soon as possible, even in cases when snakebite is only suspected.

Mild to moderate symptoms include:
- mild swelling or discoloration
- mild pain with tingling sensation at bite site
- rapid pulse
- weakness
- blurred vision
- nausea and/or vomiting
- shortness of breath.

Severe symptoms include:
- rapid swelling, numbness
- severe pain at bite site
- pinpoint pupils
- slurred speech
- shock

- convulsions
- paralysis
- unconsciousness
- no breathing or pulse.

In treating snake bite, do not
- give alcohol, sedatives, aspirin, or medications containing aspirin to relieve pain;
- apply cold compresses, ice, dry ice, chemical ice packs, spray refrigerants, or other methods of cold therapy.

Do
- have the victim lie down and keep as still and calm as possible;
- adjust the body so that the site is below the heart level;
- be alert for breathing difficulties, and begin rescue-breathing techniques if necessary;
- if pulse is not present, begin CPR immediately if you are trained in it;
- treat for shock if necessary.

For mild to moderate symptoms:
- Tie a constricting band between the bite site and the heart.
- Check for a pulse to ensure the band is not too tight.
- Adjust the bandage so fluid oozes from the wound.

Ticks: If fever, headache, and chills develop a few days after finding an attached tick, consult a doctor immediately. If you don't know how to remove a tick, do not attempt to do so; get a professional to do the job.

Insect and other critter bites and stings

Ant, bedbug, chigger (jigger), black fly, mosquito

Wash thoroughly with soap and cool water. Apply calamine lotion. For severe local reaction, make a paste of baking soda and water, and apply after washing skin with cool water.

Bee and wasp

Treat as above. Remove and discard the stinging apparatus and venom sac. If there is a severe reaction, such as difficulty in breathing, seek medical help *immediately*.

Jellyfish

When a swimmer brushes against the tentacles of a stinging jellyfish or sea nettle, the resulting sting is painful. Lightweight protective clothing, like a Lycra "swim skin" or a layer of petroleum jelly spread on bare skin, will protect against stings.

If bits or pieces of tentacles are still on the skin, pour alcohol or baby powder on the area—this will dry out the cells. If the area is painful, apply sodium bicarbonate or vinegar to the area to relieve inflammation.

Spider

Apart from some obvious exceptions, most spider bites won't be noticed beyond a little irritation or slight swelling. However, some bites can be harmful. Symptoms may include:

- severe pain
- nausea
- muscle cramps
- fever
- profuse sweating and breathing difficulties
- tingling and/or burning sensation throughout the body.

To treat harmful bites:
- Immediately seek professional medical help.

- Keep the person quiet and warm.

- Treat as for snake bite, page 96.

- Be sure the area of the bite is kept below heart level. In other words, if the bite is on the foot, don't elevate the foot above the chest.

- Watch closely for breathing difficulties.

- Begin rescue-breathing techniques if necessary.

- Place a constricting band 2–4 inches (5–10 cm) above the wound. Be sure it does not bind too tightly.

- Check for a pulse below the bite site. If a pulse is not evident, loosen the constricting band until a pulse can be felt.

- Apply a very cold, wet cloth to the affected area.

Plants to avoid

Poisoning from mushrooms, plants, or berries
Symptoms of poisoning may include: dimmed vision, cramps, vomiting, burning sensation in mouth and throat, impaired vision, and convulsions. Keep the victim warm and get medical help as soon as possible.

If possible, get the person to show you what he or she has swallowed; this information will help medical professionals.

Rashes and itching from poison ivy, poison oak, poison sumach, stinging nettles

Usually the blisters or rashes caused by these plants are uncomfortable and itchy but not life-threatening, and may not appear for 48 hours after exposure. Symptoms may include:

- a severe rash with redness
- blisters
- swelling
- burning
- itching and high fever.

To treat:

- Wash the exposed areas thoroughly with mild soap and water.
- Apply rubbing alcohol and calamine lotion.

Hot stuff

Sunburn

Most sunburn is minor, but seek medical help if the sunburn is severe, covers more than one-quarter of the body, or involves extensive blistering.

To treat:

- Apply cool compresses to the burned area to reduce pain and swelling, or take a cool shower.

- If the sunburn involves the back or an area that cannot be easily reached, soak in a tub of cool water.

- Take aspirin (if an adult) or another non-aspirin pain reliever to reduce pain.

- Apply a thin paste of baking soda and water or calamine lotion to alleviate pain.

Always wear a hat (especially important for young children and the elderly) and plenty of sunscreen. Protect eyes from the glare of the sun on the water.

- If blisters form, never break them intentionally.

- If blisters do break, apply an antibiotic ointment and cover the blisters with a sterile dressing.

Heat exhaustion/prostration

Not to be confused with sun/heat stroke, heat exhaustion starts with the accumulation of large quantities of blood in the skin. It usually occurs because of temperature conditions to which an individual is unaccustomed. Babies and small children are always more susceptible than most adults.

Symptoms may include:
- fatigue and/or irritability
- disorientation
- headache and/or faintness
- weak, rapid pulse
- shallow breathing
- dilated pupils
- cold clammy skin and/or profuse perspiration.

To treat:
- Person should lie down in a cool, shaded area or room.

- Elevate the feet.

- Massage the legs toward the heart.

- Give cold salt water (1/2 teaspoon/2 mL to 1/2 a glass of water) or cool, sweetened drinks every 15 minutes until the person recovers.

- Do not let the victim sit up, even after feeling recovered.

Even in the summer months, when it's scorching on land, the water can be cold. Keep an eye on young children playing or swimming in the water; those with blue lips should come ashore immediately.

Sunstroke (heat stroke)
Severe sunstroke is a life-threatening emergency.
Symptoms may include:
- extremely high body temperature (106° F/41° C or higher)
- hot, red, dry skin
- absence of sweating
- rapid pulse
- convulsions
- unconsciousness.

To treat:
- While waiting for or transporting to medical help, do not give any fluids.

- Lower the body temperature quickly by placing the person in a partially filled tub of cool, not cold, water.

- Briskly sponge the body until the temperature is reduced; then towel dry.

- If a tub is not available, wrap the victim in cold, wet sheets in a well-ventilated room or use fans until the body temperature is reduced.

Heat cramps
Heat cramps develop because of excessive perspiration and loss of salt from the body.
The symptoms are:
- muscle cramps, usually in the abdomen and legs
- heavy perspiration
- lightheadedness, weakness, exhaustion.
To treat: Follow the same steps as for heat exhaustion.

Cold stuff

Surviving a dunking

If the boat you are in capsizes, try to get back into the boat, or at least onto it. Unless you are an excellent swimmer and the water temperature is favorable, swimming is recommended only for short distances.

If you are unable to get back into the boat, use HELP (Heat Escape Lessening Position) until help arrives. This technique is recognized by all emergency first-aid services but works only when a lifejacket or PFD is worn.

- Fold your arms across your chest.

- Cross your ankles.

- Bring your thighs close together.

- Bend your knees.

- Try not to panic; you will last twice as long if you just hold still.

- If you have a partner, huddle with chests held close together.

Hypothermia

Here are some symptoms to watch out for and some tips on prevention and treatment. People making cross-country skiing, snowmobiling, hiking, or paddling trips should take a minute to check this section.

There are two basic types of hypothermia. In the first type, gradual exposure, steady heat loss takes place in a cold environment through respiration, evaporation (sweat, wet clothes), or inadequate insulation. Heat loss can occur during any outdoor excursion, especially in wilderness situations, where weather conditions may deteriorate unexpectedly or rapidly. Think about taking a small first-aid kit (see page 107) or a space blanket on short trips.

In the second type, acute immersion, rapid heat loss takes place in cold water, where the body cools up to 25 times faster than in air.

Faced with a cold environment, the body tries to defend itself in two ways:

- shivering, to increase muscle heat production
- blood shunting, to reduce heat loss by diverting blood flow away from the body's extremities to the body's vital organs.

Mild hypothermia occurs when the body's temperature drops below its normal 98.6° F (37° C). In the early stages, vigorous shivering is usually accompanied by increased pulse and breathing rates. Cold, white hands and feet are the first signs of blood being shunted away from the body's extremities.

In cold conditions, keep watch for symptoms in everybody—pay close attention to anybody who is confused, abnormally clumsy, paddling off-course, or otherwise behaving erratically.

Severe hypothermia is often indicated by bluish lips and fingertips, and muscular rigidity. The pulse and respiration begin to slow as the body core cools. These symptoms require urgent medical attention.

To treat mild hypothermia, if the person is conscious, talking clearly, and shivering vigorously:

- Get the person moving— physical activities generate muscle heat.
- Replace wet clothing with dry layers, covering the head and neck.
- Supply hot liquids — no alcohol.

A victim of advanced hypothermia must be treated as a medical emergency. If the person is getting stiff and is either unconscious or showing signs of clouded consciousness (slurred speech or severe loss of coordination), transport him or her to a medical facility or telephone or radio for help.

If you do not have immediate access to medical facilities:

- Remove any wet or damp clothing.

- Wrap the person warmly and transport to safety.

- If shivering has stopped, the victim has lost the ability to generate heat. You may need to use your own body to warm the person.

- Apply warmth to the neck, armpits, sides, chest, and groin and keep the head covered.

- Do not rub or stimulate the severely hypothermic patient's extremities.

Preventing hypothermia

A few commonsense tips:

- Recognize the environmental conditions leading to hypothermia.

- Wear a hat and appropriate clothing for cold and wet conditions.

- Wear polypropylene underwear to wick water away from the skin, wool on top, and a wind- and waterproof covering. Acrylic is better than wool for insulation in a dunking.

- A thermos of hot tea or chocolate will prevent the onset of mild hypothermia.

- In wilderness settings, carry matches in a waterproof container and some form of improvisational shelter.

- Learn to recognize the early warning signs of hypothermia.

Wearing a good sunscreen and a hat is as important in winter as in summer. The glare from the sun on snow or water is very strong. Wear good sunglasses.

Frostbite
If on an outing, check one another for frostbite.
Symptoms are:
- Skin that is white and has a "wooden" feel all the way through. The degree of paleness will vary according to the skin tone.
- Numbness.

To treat superficial frostbite:
- Rewarm by placing the area against a warm body part.

To treat deep frostbite while getting medical help:
- Remove constricting clothing.
- Immerse the affected part in a warm-water bath of 105°–110° F (40°–43° C) and continue to monitor the water temperature. Add more warm water as needed.
- Do not use dry heat to rewarm as it cannot be effectively maintained at 105°–110°F and can cause burns, further damaging the tissues.
- The affected part should be immersed for 25–40 minutes.
- The rewarmed part should be wrapped and protected from movement until assessed.

Eyelashes freezing together
Put hand over eye until ice melts, then gently open the eye.

Snowblindness
Eye protection from the sun is just as necessary on cloudy or overcast days as it is in full sunlight. Snow blindness can even occur during a snowstorm if the cloud cover is thin.

To prevent sunburn of the eyes:
- Wear good sunglasses with side shields or goggles.

Symptoms, which occur 8–12 hours after exposure are:
- Eyes feel dry and irritated, then feel as if they are full of sand.
- Moving or blinking eyes becomes extremely painful, as is exposure to light.
- Eyelids may swell, eyes become red, and excessive tearing occurs.

To treat:
- Do not rub the eyes.
- Place a cold compress on the eyes and stay in a dark environment until you can get medical help.

First-aid kits

There are many different types of prepackaged first-aid kits available commercially. Many are tailored for specific conditions such as mountaineering or trekking. Here are some minimum requirements for a vacation home kit.

Antibiotic ointment: For topical application on minor cuts and abrasions.

Antihistamine: Useful as a decongestant for colds and allergies, and for relief from the effects of insect bites or stings. *Antihistamines can cause drowsiness and interact with alcohol, so care should be taken when using them.*

Antiseptic: For cleaning cuts and grazes.

Calamine lotion or cream: For relief from itching and sunburn.

Decongestant tablets: For nasal congestion due to colds, allergies, or water sports.

Hydrocortisone cream: For topical relief of itching due to insect bites or sunburn.

Insect repellent: There are many varieties. Discuss with your local pharmacist what's most suitable for your area. With recent increased concern about Lyme disease, skin and clothing repellents are available for protection against ticks.

Kits should be kept in airtight containers, such as a Zip-lock bag. Replace any items that have been used. Keep an eye on expiry dates. Keep your first-aid manual nearby.

Oil of cloves: Always useful for unexpected toothache.

Pain-relief medications: Aspirin, Tylenol, or Ibuprofen (Advil, Nuprin) for general relief of minor aches and pains.

Sunscreen: Any brand with an SPF greater than 15.

General medical supplies: In addition to the above, a kit should contain:

- Butterfly dressings (good for keeping a wound closed)
- Cotton wool
- Elastic bandage
- Extra-large sterile dressings
- Gauze bandage
- Gauze pads
- Individually wrapped sterile adhesive dressings
- Latex gloves
- Safety pins
- Scissors
- Sterile eye pad
- Tape
- Thermometer
- Triangular bandage
- Tweezers

Emergency supplies

Consider keeping an emergency cache in the cottage or chalet that includes some of the following items:
- Chemical light stick or Beta light (light-emitting crystal)
- Water rations
- Emergency space blanket (these are sold at most camping stores)
- 200-calorie bars
- String
- Candles and matches (keep in waterproof container)
- Antibiotic ointment
- Adhesive bandages
- If your cottage is very isolated, you might want some signal flares.

For short trips: Consider taking a small, portable emergency kit that can be kept in a backpack or fanny belt. Camping stores sell small, solid fuel tablets in their own stove containers. Other items might include:
- 200-calorie bars
- Chemical light stick
- Emergency space blanket
- Individually wrapped adhesive dressings
- Matches (keep in waterproof container)
- Pocket knife
- Safety pins
- Signal flare

This is a good place to record favorite picnic spots, hiking trails, beaches, restaurants, amusement parks, etc. On your maps be sure to indicate "No Trespassing" areas for hikers and ATV users, and water hazards for boaters.

Our Favorite Summer Day Trips

Where we keep our printed maps of the area, compass, etc.:

....

Day trips on foot:

....

....

....

....

....

....

....

....

....

....

....

....

Day trips by boat:

Day trips by car:

....

....

....

....

....

....

....

....

....

....

....

....

....

....

....

....

Day trips by ATV:

Outdoor Games

Badminton

Rackets, shuttlecocks, and net are kept in:

....

Basic rules:

Most of us simply bash the birdie back and forth and see how long we can keep it going across the net. But for those rule-oriented sorts who like to mark off the court with rope so that they know when the shuttlecock is "in" or "out," the court is 44 feet (13 m) long and 20 feet (6 m) across. A short service line is drawn across the court 6-1/2 feet (2 m) back from each side of the 5-foot (1.5-m)-high net.

To begin a proper game, one player serves from behind the short service line diagonally across the court to his or her opponent. The birdie must land beyond the other player's short service line but inside the side and back lines. If the player's shuttlecock falls out of bounds, the other player serves. If it looks as though it will fall within bounds, the opposing player tries to hit it back across the net. The shuttlecock is allowed to touch the net, but the racket is not. Only the server wins points, and 15 points are required to win a set. Two sets must be won to win a game.

Croquet

Hoops and mallets are kept in:

....

Basic rules:

Older children have been known to make this game into a cross between miniature golf and hardball by setting up impossible courses in the woods. However, wooden balls ricocheting off rocks can blacken eyes and other body parts, so in the interests of safety, here's how a regular course is set up on flat ground:

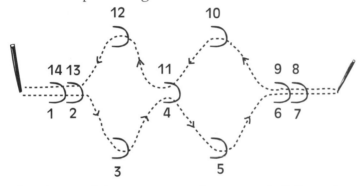

The object of the game is to drive your ball from the starting post through wickets 1 to 7, strike the turning post, return through wickets 8 to 14, and strike the starting post.

At the start of play, the ball is placed one-third of the distance between the starting post and the first wicket. A player receives an extra shot for each wicket his or her ball rolls through and two extra shots if an opponent's ball is hit. If you strike an opponent's ball, you can choose to use one of your shots to "croquet" the struck ball. This is done by placing your ball against your opponent's, putting one foot on your ball, and striking it (the ball, not your foot!) with the mallet. The impact, if you're lucky, will send your opponent's ball rolling off the course. Players receive a single shot after striking the turning post. The first person to finish the course and hit the starting post is the winner.

Horseshoes

Horseshoes and pegs are located:

....

Basic rules
The object of this simple game is to pitch a horseshoe with an underhand throw so that it lands around a stake or closer to it than your opponent's horseshoe. Each player pitches two horseshoes per turn. A "ringer" earns a player 3 points while a "leaner" is worth 1 point. Horseshoes that touch the stake or are within 6 inches (15 cm) of the stake also score one point. If both your horseshoes fall nearer to the stake than your opponent's, 2 points are added to your score. The game is over when one player accumulates 50 points.

Golf

Location of local courses:

....

....

....

....

....

....

....

Volleyball

Ball and net are kept in:

....

Basic rules

If you want to mark off a court with rope, the playing area is roughly 60 feet (18 m) long and 30 feet (9 m) across. The height of the net is about 8 feet (2 m). The game can be played with two to six players per team.

To begin a game, the server on one team stands behind the end line on the right-hand third of the court. He or she serves the ball, using an underhand serve. The other team tries to hit it back. If they fail, their opponents win a point and serve again. Only the serving team wins points. A player can't catch or hit the ball twice but can pass it to a teammate. If the ball isn't hit over the net by the third pass, the opposing team wins the serve. The ball can hit the net during play but not when it is being served. A game is 15 points.

Closing-Up Checklist for Guests

In addition to power, heating, and plumbing instructions, don't forget to mention garbage disposal, pulling up boats, putting away boating equipment and lawn chairs, covering the barbecue, closing gates, and where the key is left.

Closing-Up in the Fall

A fall list is included for those times when you are unable to tackle this chore yourself.

123

Winter Use

Opening-up checklist

Closing-up checklist

Winter Sports

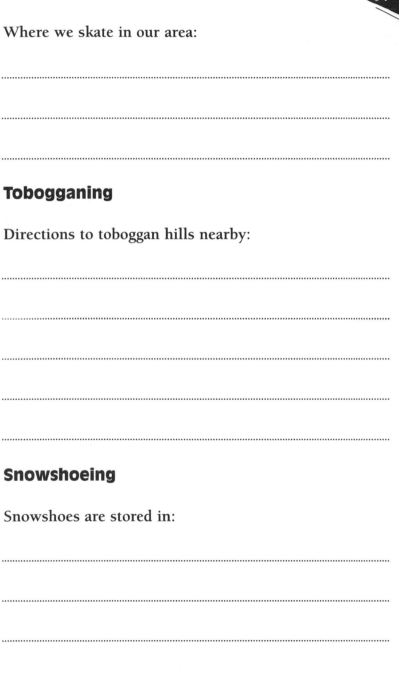

Skating

Where we skate in our area:

....

....

....

Tobogganing

Directions to toboggan hills nearby:

....

....

....

....

Snowshoeing

Snowshoes are stored in:

....

....

....

....

Cross-country skiing

Cross-country skis and wax are stored in:

....

....

Snowmobiling

Directions for operating our snowmobile:

....

....

....

....

....

....

....

....

....

....

....

Safety tips

- Wear sensible, protective clothing designed for snowmobiling.
- Use a full-sized helmet with goggles or visor.
- Avoid wearing long scarves. They may get caught in moving parts of the snowmobile.
- Always use the buddy system.
- Children under 12 should not operate a snowmobile. In some jurisdictions, kids 12 through 15 years of age may operate a snowmobile only if they hold a safety certificate.
- Know the weather forecast before you set out on a long trip.
- Ride safe, ride sober.

Rules in our area:

....

....

....

It's probably a good idea to ask your guests to stay off the ice on snowmobiles even if they see other snowmobilers traveling on it. Locals are familiar with ice conditions on different parts of the lake, but it's difficult to give guests accurate directions because conditions can vary from day to day.

Care of the environment

- Where snowmobiles may be operated in our province or state:

....

- Don't operate the snowmobile when there is not enough snow cover to protect ground vegetation.
- Be litter conscious.
- Do not chase wild animals.
- Honor all "no trespassing" signs.

Our Favorite Winter Day Trips

Where we keep our printed maps of the area:

....

Day trips on cross-country skis:

....

....

....

....

....

....

....

....

....

....

....

....

....

Day trips by snowmobile:

....

....

....

....

....

....

....

....

....

....

....

....

....

....

....

....

Day trips to downhill ski areas:

Cottage Bookshelf

Magazines
Cottage Life Magazine, 111 Queen Street. E., Ste. 408, Toronto, Ontario M5C 1S2.

Books
Bennet, Doug, and Tim Tiner. *Up North*. Toronto: Reed Books, 1993.

Burns, Max. *Cottage Water Systems*. Toronto: Cottage Life Books, 1993.

Canadian Coast Guard. *Safe Boating Guide*. Ottawa: Minister of Supply and Services Canada, 1994.

Caswell, Christopher. *The Illustrated Book of Basic Boating*. New York: Hearst Marine Books, 1990.

Drake, Jane, and Ann Love. *The Kids Cottage Book*. Toronto: Kids Can Press, 1993.

Edwards, Frank B., ed. *The Cottage Book: A Collection of Practical Advice*. Newburgh, Ont.: Hedgehog Productions, 1991

Lockhart, Gary. *The Weather Companion*. New York: John Wiley & Sons, 1988.

Morehead, Albert H. *The New Complete Hoyle: The Authoritative Guide to the Official Rules of All Popular Games of Skill and Chance*. New York: Doubleday, 1991.

Ontario Ministry of Environment and Energy. *Care and Feeding of Your Septic System*. Toronto: Ontario Ministry of Environment and Energy, n.d.

Peterson, Roger Tory, ed. *The Peterson Field Guide Series*. Boston: Houghton Mifflin.

Phillips, Bob. *The Cottager's Handbook*. Scarborough, Ont.: Prentice-Hall Canada, 1987.

Phillips, David. *The Day Niagara Falls Ran Dry! Canadian Weather Facts and Trivia.* Toronto: Key Porter Books, 1993.

Reader's Digest. *How to Do Just About Anything.* Pleasantville, NY: Reader's Digest Association, 1986.

Thomas, Dirk. *Harrowsmith Country Life Guide to Wood Heat.* Charlotte, VT: Camden House, 1992.

Veffer, Carolynne, and Wendy Thomas. *Bluffle: The Biographical Dictionary Game.* Toronto: GameBooks, 1994.

Wiseman, John. *Collins Gem SAS Survival Guide.* Toronto: HarperCollins, 1993.

Web sites to check out at home
Bat Conservation International
http://www.batcon.org/batinfo.html

BUGNET http://frost2.flemingc.on.ca/~pbell/welcome.html

Environment Canada Weather Reports http://www.doe.ca/

HearthNet http://hearth.com/hearthnet.html

Home Maintenance and Repair Page, Michigan State University
http://lep.cl.msu.edu/msueimp/htdoc/mod02/
master02.html

Septic Systems Website http://www1.mhv.net/~dfriedman/sept-book.htm

Your Weather Bureau On-Line (US)
http://www.crl.com/~rfellure/ronsweat.html

Guest Log

Date:

Date:

Date:

Date

Date:

Date:

Date:

Date:

Date:

140

Date:

Date:

Date:

141

Date:

Date:

Date:

Date:

Date:

Date:

Date:

Date:

Date:

Date:

Date:

Date:

Date:

Date:

Date:

146

Date:

Date:

Date:

Date:

Date:

Date:

Date:

Date:

Date:

149

Date:

Date:

Date:

Date:

Date:

Date:

Date:

Date:

Date:

Date:

Date:

Date:

153

Date:

....

....

....

....

....

Date:

....

....

....

....

....

Date:

....

....

....

....

....

Date:

Date:

Date:

Date:

Date:

Date:

Date:

Date:

Date:

Date:

Date:

Date:

158

Date:

Date:

Date:

PAULA CHABANAIS is the perfect cottage guest. In England, she once ran a B&B in Cornwall and a small camp for teenagers, loves kids and dogs, knows first-aid and is a fantastic cook. When not visiting friends' cottages, she runs Paula Chabanais & Associates, a Toronto-based print-management consulting group.

LAURIE COULTER, a Toronto writer and editor, is a lifelong cottager. Her family has rented, built, bought, and shared cottages from Lake Huron to the Kawarthas. She and her brother now own the family cottage in Haliburton. Over the years, she has played an active role on the executive of their lake's cottagers' association.

PETER MAHER's skills as a carpenter and cook make him a welcome guest at his friends' cottages. An award-winning designer, he has renovated houses ranging from a Victorian house in Toronto to a farmhouse in Provence. He is also a dedicated canoeist and backpacker.

Paula, Laurie and Peter are partners in Russet Books, the creators of *The Paddler's Journal & Companion*, published by Doubleday Canada Limited.